The Road to Bethlehem

An Advent Prayer and Devotional Guide

Leanna Lindsey Hollis M.D.

Pinion Press
Blue Springs MS
2013

Library of Congress Control Number

Hollis, Leanna Lindsey
The Road to Bethlehem: An Advent Prayer Guide. Experiencing the Christmas Story in a New and Prayerful way/Leanna Lindsey Hollis M.D.

ISBN 978-0-9770201-3-3

Published by Pinion Press
1754 CR 278, Suite 102
Blue Springs, MS 38828

Printed in the United States

Dedication:

*Every word that has been written was done with my
precious son Ryan in mind.*

*Dear one, this is for you.
I love you.*

Preface

When I started this little Advent book, it was early August 2013. These were the daily devotionals sent to the Parents of Prodigals group. We were (and still are) praying daily for our children and loved ones. We used these little prayer starters to help us pray in agreement, trusting that God honors those prayers, even when separated by hundreds of miles.

I never intended to write an Advent guide. It just happened. We didn't pray it in quite this order, but I have rearranged it to follow along with the story in Luke. Up front, I have to tell you that there are forty-three devotionals. Since there wasn't a plan at the start, it just happened that way. If you want to read one a day before Christmas, you will have to start on November 13th. If you want to arrive at the birth of Jesus on Christmas day, you might prefer to start November 23rd and continue on after Christmas.

However you choose to use this little volume, I pray it will be as much of a blessing to you and your family as the writing of it has been to me.

May this be the Christmas you are overwhelmed with the love of Christ, humbled by the Gift of God, and forever changed by His Grace.

Blessings,

Leanna Hollis

Table of Contents

1

*Just as they were handed down to us by those who from the
beginning were eyewitnesses and servants of the word,
(Luke 1:2 NASB)
In the beginning was the Word, and the Word was with
God, and the Word was God. And the Word became flesh,
and dwelt among us, and we saw His glory, glory as of the
only begotten from the Father, full of grace and truth.
(John 1:1, 14 NASB)
Your word I have treasured in my heart, That I may not sin
against You. (Psalms 119:11 NASB)*

Luke describes two previous levels of information
about Jesus. The first accounts came from eyewitnesses and
"servants of the word", who handed down, probably orally,
the stories of their personal experience with Christ. Luke
makes a clear distinction between eyewitnesses and
servants of the word. Eyewitnesses simply reported what
they had seen just as they had seen it. They had a story to
tell, but not much more.

Servants of the word, however, are a different
matter. The term servant implies one who obeys the
command of a master. We easily understand the term
"servant of God" or "servant of Caesar", but "servant of the
word" doesn't seem quite so clear-cut. John tells us that
Jesus is the Word, and Peter, when asked if he wanted to
leave Jesus as the crowds had done, proclaimed, "Where
would we go? You have words of eternal life!" (John 6:68)
How amazing!

Jesus IS the Word.
Jesus HAS the Word.
Jesus SPOKE the Word.

Our job is to know the Word, embrace the Word, and incorporate it into our lives in such a way that we become SERVANTS of the Word.

Eyewitnesses are observers who have a story to tell. Servants of the Word are more than observers. They have become participants who give evidence of the truth of their story by their changed lives. Which are you? Do you merely pass along the stories of Jesus you learned as a child or are you a participant who demonstrates truth by the power of your changed life?

Today pray to become a more committed Servant of the Word. Pray, too, that our loved ones will encounter believers who are Servants of the Word, bearing irrefutable witness to the power of Christ by the quality of their transformed lives. May they present that truth in such a way that it is irresistible.

...So you can know beyond the shadow of a doubt the reliability of what you were taught. (Luke 1:4 MSG)

Luke explained the purpose of his writing. Although many people had attempted to compile an account of the life of Christ, he was writing based on his own intense investigation of the truth. Perhaps he was the kind of physician who needed a double-blind controlled study to be certain of the facts. He admits that he "investigated everything". He is writing from certainty, not doubt, based on facts he has assembled, not just hearsay.

Luke carefully investigated all the accounts about Jesus, and wrote a report of his findings (the gospel of Luke) for Theophilus. His stated purpose was so that Theophilus could "know beyond a shadow of doubt" the reliability of what he had been taught about Jesus.

Understanding truth without doubt should make a significant difference in our lifestyle and our priorities, shouldn't it? Pray today that we and our loved ones will be confronted with truth in a way that removes all doubt and results in life-altering change.

They were both righteous in the sight of God, walking blamelessly in all the commandments and requirements of the Lord. But they had no child, because Elizabeth was barren, and they were both advanced in years. (Luke 1:6, 7 NASB)

Like most young Jewish couples, Zacharias and Elizabeth had asked God for a child. With every passing year of barrenness, they asked. Finally they reached the "senior citizen" years, and still no child. It seemed obvious to most people that God had said no to their request. There may have been tears and heartache, but this remarkable couple was not embittered. Instead, they lived righteous, blameless lives, serving God just the way they always had.

Finally, two amazing things happened. First, Zacharias was chosen by lot to enter the temple and burn incense. Second, on that remarkable incense day, an angel appeared and told Zacharias that his prayers had been heard and they would have a son. What??? Zacharias was stunned and doubtful and, in his unbelief, he was struck mute for months.

Then, a third amazing thing happened. The son was actually born. What a son! John was the forerunner of Christ and would be a righteous man with a tremendous ministry in Israel. Can't you just imagine their joy? Their son was worth the wait.

Some of us have been asking God for our loved ones to be redeemed by the blood of the Lamb for decades, and may well be weary in the asking. Weary does not mean defeated, nor does delay mean God will not move. It may mean He has prepared an answer for you that is so stunningly wonderful that it will make all the delay worth the wait. Can you wait blamelessly for His answer? Will you?

Pray today for our loved ones to be redeemed no matter how long it takes and pray for us all to have the grace to wait blamelessly, regardless of the duration of that wait.

And an angel of the Lord appeared to him, standing to the right of the altar of incense. (Luke 1:11 NASB)
When He had taken the book, the four living creatures and the twenty-four elders fell down before the Lamb, each one holding a harp and golden bowls full of incense, which are the prayers of the saints. (Revelation 5:8 NASB)

In the temple, there was a golden altar that measured 1x 1 x 2 cubits (roughly 18 x 18 x 36 inches) made of acacia wood and overlaid with gold. There were horns on each corner with rings for carrying poles on the sides. This altar of incense stood at the entrance to the Holy of Holies that contained the ark and the mercy seat where God met with His people. A golden bowl of incense was perpetually burning there before The Lord, and it was changed out twice a day. In order to reach the mercy seat, the priest had to pass the altar of incense and walk through the sweet fragrance of the incense burning there.

On this amazing day, Zacharias had been chosen to burn incense on the golden altar. As he was standing in front of the veil that separated him from the mercy seat, an angel appeared to him with the astounding news that his prayers had been answered and he would have a son.

The angel was not there because it was the only place he could catch Zacharias's attention. The appearance of the angel in this particular place was highly significant. The Revelation describes the twenty four elders bowing before the throne of God, and holding golden bowls full of incense. The incense is the prayers of the saints.

The incense Zacharias was burning before The Lord was not just to make the room smell nice. It was symbolic of the prayers of God's faithful followers. Zacharias was symbolically placing the prayers he and Elizabeth had prayed on the altar and burning them as an offering to God. He was symbolically giving all he had longed for and prayed for back to God. It's not surprising, then, that the angel appeared to say that the very prayers he had just put on the altar had been answered.

It's amazing to think that our prayers are like a sweet smelling incense before The Lord. It's even more amazing to think that, just like in the temple, it is through the sweet fragrance of our prayers that we approach the presence of God. Because the sacrifice of Jesus on the cross ripped the veil that separated us from the mercy seat, you and I can be a kind of Zacharias as we approach God through the incense that is our prayers for our loved ones. He delights in our prayers.

Today, take heart in the fact that you, dear one, have been chosen by God Himself through Christ to bring the incense of prayer before Him. Lift your prayers with confidence, knowing that you kneel before the mercy seat of God. As you do, pray for surrender, salvation, and transformation for our loved ones as well as for ourselves.

It is he who will go as a forerunner before Him in the spirit and power of Elijah, to turn the hearts of the fathers back to the children, and the disobedient to the attitude of the righteous, so as to make ready a people prepared for the Lord." (Luke 1:17 NASB)

His life's work was assigned before John was born. He was to prepare God's people for the coming Messiah. He would go before Jesus in the spirit and power of Elijah, and his preaching would turn the hearts of fathers to their sons, and the disobedient to the attitude of the righteous. What a job!!

He was not to preach sermons designed to comfort the grieving or encourage the downtrodden. He was to preach restoration of relationship and repentance of the rebellious, and only those topics. No other sermons would do, because right relationships and humble, repentant hearts are needed to be right with Christ.

Today, let's pray the "work of John" for ourselves and our loved ones. Pray for healing and restoration of any relationships that are fractured, as well as repentance for the rebellious. Pray that our loved ones will be prepared spiritually to respond to Christ with open, willing hearts.

Now in the sixth month the angel Gabriel was sent from God to a city in Galilee called Nazareth, to a virgin engaged to a man whose name was Joseph, of the descendants of David; and the virgin's name was Mary. And coming in, he said to her, "Greetings, favored one! The Lord is with you." (Luke 1:26-28 NASB)

What a surprise it was for a barely-into-her-teens girl to have a visit from Gabriel, an angel straight from the presence of God! How much more surprising to hear that she was not only favored by God but chosen by Him!

These verses tell us quite a bit about Mary... Virgin and pleasing to God tell us that, even at her young age, she was making right choices and had a heart for righteousness. Pleasing God did not happen by chance. It came as a result of one right choice after another.

How easy it would have been to indulge in teenage rebellion and negate the plan God had for her! How easy it would have been to miss the joy God had set for her! When Mary was making those right choices, she had no idea what God was orchestrating, no idea where her choices would lead. Like every young girl, there were undoubtedly times when a wrong choice would have been more fun or more convenient, yet she persevered in righteousness.

There is no way in advance to know where our choices will lead us or how they will limit what God has planned for us, but it is clear from Scripture that our choices matter and that they affect our future.

As you look at your own choices and the path on which they have led you, pray that our loved ones will look at the results of the choices they have already made and begin to make choices for righteousness that are pleasing to God.

*And behold, you will conceive in your womb and bear a
son, and you shall name Him Jesus. He will be great and
will be called the Son of the Most High; and the Lord God
will give Him the throne of His father David; and He will
reign over the house of Jacob forever, and His kingdom
will have no end." Mary said to the angel, "How can this
be, since I am a virgin?" ...
For nothing will be impossible with God." (Luke 1:31-34,
37 NASB)*

Mary must have been terrified just to see Gabriel.
When he started talking, her terror must have become
astronomic. The angel told her she would conceive a child
and then told her all about her Son-to-come. He told her
wonderful things like "throne of David" and "kingdom will
have no end", but Mary hung on those first few words.
"You will conceive" and thought, "No. That's not right.
Can't be. Impossible!" Mary knew who she was and how
she had lived. She knew that what the angel said about
conceiving was impossible. She didn't even bother to
address how likely it was that her son would become
king.

It's interesting though, that she does not say its not
going to happen or that she doesn't want it to happen. All
she asks is "how can it happen?" The angel tells her the
most beautiful words. "Nothing will be impossible with
God."

Nothing

There is nothing so difficult or so unlikely that God
cannot accomplish it. He who can create a child with His
essence can transform a child by the power of His Spirit.

Pray today that God will transform our loved ones in such a way that the impossible happens and our loved ones become more than we ever imagined they could be.

For nothing will be impossible with God."
(Luke 1:37 NASB)

My early childhood church held revivals once a year. I remember the choir leading out in every service with the same spirited song.

> *"Nothing is impossible*
> *When you put your trust in God.*
> *Nothing is impossible*
> *When you're trusting in His*
> *Word.*
> *Hearken to the voice of God to thee,*
> *"Is there anything too hard for Me?"*
> *So put your trust in God alone,*
> *And rest upon His Word,*
> *For everything, yes everything*
> *is possible with God!"*

Eugene Clark was the wise man who wrote these words, and I've since wondered why we don't sing them every week. Better yet, every day. Why is it that we only expect and look for the miraculous during special services?

I'm personally inclined to look for a miracle every day. When we have our spiritual eyes open for evidence of God at work, demonstrating His power, we are never disappointed, and are frequently stunned by what He does. People often ask me to "say a little prayer" for their need. I always think, "You surely don't want a little answer. Let's pray something big!" One of the reasons I recognize the miraculous is that, somewhere along my way, I began to pray the biggest prayer I can think of and ask God to exceed that.

Specific prayers help me to recognize God at work. If I ask God to provide for the needs of the music ministry at our church, He will respond to that prayer, but His answer may be less obvious. If I ask Him to provide four new microphones through special donations to the music ministry and do it in the next few weeks, and He does, I'm thrilled and in awe. I know He responded specifically to the specific prayer I prayed.

Now, the prayers here are not just prayers that are made up for some great effect or to impress the hearers. Speaking the prayer God wants to answer is critical to seeing Him move. How? The key to knowing what God wants to do is being still long enough to hear that Still Small Voice and quiet enough to recognize it. Time in the Word through Bible study is key. Praying Scripture is a good way to pray something we know God approves.

Forming prayers that bring glory to God with the answer (and even better, keep us completely out of the spotlight) are vital. The point of answered prayer is not to make us look good for getting God to do something. The point is for us to agree with Him in prayer (not convince Him to agree with us) so that He can get the glory and honor and credit when He moves.

With all that in mind, pray the biggest prayer you can think of today for our loved ones. Don't just pray they will stop doing something, pray for conviction, repentance, brokenness, surrender, transformation, and service. Pray that God will use what He does in the lives of our loved ones to bring glory to Himself and cause thousands of people to be drawn back to Him. Maybe millions of people.

Pray they will become the most godly people you know.

Years ago, three women decided to pray for God to move in the worst person they knew who needed God the most... And I was that person. In response to those impossible prayers, He brought, repentance, brokenness, surrender, transformation, and service. The gospel has been shared with literally thousands of people over the years. All because three women dared to ask God to do the impossible! What will God do in response to YOUR prayers?

And Mary said, "Behold, the bondslave of the Lord; may it be done to me according to your word." And the angel departed from her. (Luke 1:38 NASB)

Mary was wise beyond her years. Scripture doesn't say that, but we can deduce that from the fact that Jehovah trusted her with His Only Son. She was obviously bright enough to ask sensible questions in the presence of an angel. When her questions were done, however, she did not respond with "what-if's". What if Joseph or my parents don't believe me? What if Joseph puts me away and the community turns against me? She addresses none of the things that would worry most young Jewish girls.

Instead, she responds with total surrender. Whatever God wants for her is what she wants. It's a frightening, severe kind of faith, this relinquishing of control. For Mary, it brought heartache and devastating loss, but it also brought joy beyond measure. That faith would sustain her the rest of her life and undoubtedly shape the earthly life of our Savior.

Sometimes, the fear of God's plan keeps us from Him. The dread that He will force us to do whatever is our worst nightmare - in job, relationship, sacrifice - causes us to keep Him at arm's length.

Pray today that neither we nor our loved ones would miss God's plan because of fear or dislike of His plan, but that we would respond to His call with the surrender of the young Jewish girl.

And Mary said, "Behold, the bondslave of the Lord; may it be done to me according to your word." And the angel departed from her. (Luke 1:38 NASB)
..."Father, if You are willing, remove this cup from Me; yet not My will, but Yours be done." (Luke 22:42 NASB)

From the moment the angel spoke to Mary, she demonstrated a complete surrender to the will of God. It was not surrender born in the glow of an angelic visitation but must have been a way of life that she continued to demonstrate before her children. Jesus, in the garden prayers before His arrest, demonstrated that same degree of self-sacrificing surrender. "Not my will, but Thine be done." It was the same unfailing obedience He had seen in His mother.

How wonderful it would be to exhibit the faith and surrender of Mary before our loved ones and see it bear fruit in their lives! Despite the frailties of our flesh, we have walked out our faith, albeit imperfectly, before those closest to us.

Pray today that, when decision time comes to our loved ones, they will recall our obedience rather than our failure, our love for our Lord rather than our fear, and that they will be empowered with an even greater degree of surrender to the will of God.

And blessed is she who believed that there would be a fulfillment of what had been spoken to her by the Lord."
(Luke 1:45 NASB)

On Mary's arrival, John leapt for joy in his mother's womb. It was a confirmation for Elizabeth of what she already knew - probably by divine revelation - that Mary was carrying the Messiah. Some commentators believe that this next verse "blessed is she who believed" refers to Mary, but I think Elizabeth might have been referring to herself.

Perhaps, during the years of praying for a child, she had heard the quiet voice of God assuring her that she would, one day, have a child and, despite all odds and in the face of certain impossibility, she had continued to believe "what has been spoken to her by The Lord". At last, she was seeing the plan of God unfold and she was filled with the joy of answered prayers and completed promises.

If you have a promise from God concerning your loved one (and Scripture is filled with them) do not despair at a delay in fulfillment. Elizabeth is proof that the answer can still come. Hold to what God has promised and choose to believe Him, no matter the odds. What joy and blessing will be yours when His answer comes! Finally seeing the answer to your prayers is a priceless gift, and worth the wait.

"For He has had regard for the humble state of His bondslave... (Luke 1:48 NASB)

When Elizabeth and Mary met, they both broke out in spontaneous praise to God. One of Mary's first statements of praise says "He has regarded the humble state of His bondslave." Mary was saying that God had noticed her right where she was, despite her poverty, her low status as a woman, and her insignificance in the world. El Roi (the God who sees) had His eye on her.

He is still El Roi and he still sees the most insignificant people, the most rebellious, and the most unworthy. Take heart in the fact that El Roi sees. He sees you and your loved ones. He knows their "humble state" and is willing to receive then to Himself.

Pray today that our loved ones will sense the ever-seeing, ever-knowing presence of God and respond with the surrender and praise of Mary.

"For the Mighty One has done great things for me; And holy is His name. (Luke 1:49 NASB)
"Offer to God a sacrifice of thanksgiving And pay your vows to the Most High; Call upon Me in the day of trouble; I shall rescue you, and you will honor Me." (Psalms 50:14, 15 NASB)

Little Jewish boys were taught, and memorized, the five books of law. Little girls were taught, and memorized, Psalms and Proverbs. How very appropriate to give the poetry to the ones who were the "heart" of the home. The other great gift the Psalms provided those young girls was lessons in prayer and how to deal with trouble.

Psalm 50 teaches that, when we are in a time of trouble, we should offer a sacrifice of thanksgiving to God, right in the midst of that trouble. We are not to wait until the trouble passes. Right where we are, in the midst of dire circumstances, we are to give thanks. It takes a grateful heart to find things for which to thank God when the future looks bleak and you don't know what to do next. Thanking God when your earthly life hangs in the balance as a result of God's blessing is especially hard.

If a virgin who willingly had relations with a man was discovered, both the man and the virgin were to be put to death by stoning. Perhaps the lack of a human partner was a protection, but as her pregnancy became apparent, Mary was quite literally escaping a death sentence by visiting Elizabeth. Most young girls would have been terrified.

Mary, however, must have taken those lessons in Psalms to heart. Her response to Elizabeth's reference to her pregnancy was pure thanksgiving. It was a pure sacrifice of thanksgiving, as she not only thanked God in the midst of her trial, but she also thanked Him for her trial.

She did what she had been taught from Scripture and the result was exactly what Scripture promised. God not only rescued her, but used her response to her circumstances to bring honor and glory to His name.

Wow! God did exactly what He said He **would** do when Mary did exactly what He said **to** do! How marvelous is that? If we believed Scripture enough to actually obey completely, perhaps we would see more Scripture promises fulfilled.

A time when our loved ones are barreling down the wide road of destruction and ruin hardly seems the best time for which to give thanks to God. It seems, however, that it is exactly the time for which we should give thanks! It is not that we rejoice because of their wrong choices, but because nothing is impossible with God. He sees and knows even the number of hairs on their heads. He knows their name. He is not willing for them to perish. It is His desire that they come to repentance. He can, and does respond to the prayers of His people.

Today, offer a sacrifice of thanksgiving for your circumstances and that of your loved ones. Thank God for how He is working in it, how He will use it, how He will rescue from it, and He will use it to bring honor and glory to His name.

"He has given help to Israel His servant, In remembrance of His mercy." (Luke 1:54 NASB)

Israel was under Roman rule, and Roman soldiers stood ready to enforce Roman law on the Jewish people. They were in their homeland, but they were not free. God's people needed help.

Mary rightly discerned that God had sent help to Israel. What is amazing about the help God sent is that it arrived in the form of a pregnant teenaged girl and a soon-to-be-newborn baby. It looked so little like help that most people missed it.

Pray today that God will send His unlikely aid to our loved ones and that, recognized or not, our Lord will draw them back to Himself.

Pray too that they will embrace the infant Savior who became our risen Redeemer with their heart and life.

"He has given help to Israel His servant, In remembrance of His mercy, (Luke 1:54 NASB)

The help God sent was in the form of a pregnant girl and a newborn babe. What more vulnerable form could He choose? The Merriam-Webster online dictionary defines vulnerable as:

1:capable of being physically or emotionally wounded 2 : open to attack or damage : assailable <vulnerable to criticism. Synonyms include helpless, defenseless, powerless, weak.

That pretty well sums up the position God chose in His unlikely vessels, and it so aptly describes us as humans. Despite all the defenses we construct and the schemes we devise, our strength comes from God or it doesn't come at all.

Mary's job was to allow God to create in her and work through her at her most vulnerable. The Babe Jesus arrived so very vulnerable but filled with the Spirit, and His job was to grow and to obey. He did not come to fight military conquerors or eliminate evil from the world. He came as the spotless Lamb of God and His job was to stay spotless and offer Himself as a sacrifice of grace. If we could emulate those two Helpers of God, we would be well on our way to pleasing Him.

Today, pray that we will allow God to work through us and that we will work hard to remain spotless and offer ourselves as vessels of grace to a lost and dying world.

"Blessed be the Lord God of Israel, For He has visited us and accomplished redemption for His people, (Luke 1:68 NASB)

400 years had passed from the time of Malachi until that of Matthew. God had promised redemption but all those years of silence were pretty discouraging. When Zacharias's speech was restored, his first words were praise and prophesy.

..."He has accomplished redemption..."

The forerunner John was only a few days old and the Savior Jesus had not yet been born. Redemption under construction, maybe, but accomplished? It is hard to see, but Zacharias was speaking truth. When God says He will do something, He will. We can count on it. When God begins something, He will finish it. We can count on that, too. Philippians 1:6 reminds us that He does (and will) complete what He begins.

As we pray for our loved ones today, remember to thank God for the hope of completion and continue to pray that He will complete what He has begun in their lives.

To grant us that we, being rescued from the hand of our enemies, Might serve Him without fear, In holiness and righteousness before Him all our days. (Luke 1:74, 75 NASB)

This is a picture of redemption:

Rescued from the hold of our enemy, the evil one

Serving our Lord without fear, in holiness, and in righteousness

Is that not a beautiful picture of that for which we long for our loved ones?

Pray today for redemption that begins with rescue from the bondage of sin and is demonstrated by holy, righteous service.

...Because of the tender mercy of our God, With which the Sunrise from on high will visit us, To shine upon those who sit in darkness and the shadow of death, To guide our feet into the way of peace." (Luke 1:78, 79 NASB)

Zacharias's prophecy continued. Because God has such a tender heart, He did not want to give us the hell and damnation we deserve for our sins. Instead He sent the Sunrise from on high (His only Son, Jesus) to come to us. The soon-to-be-born Jesus will shine His light in the darkness for those who are sitting there. Whether they are sitting in darkness by choice or because they are not able to find their way out and have given up, His light will shine on them.

The darkness does not frighten Him or intimidate Him. Those in darkness are not lost to our Lord. He knows where they are and how to get to them. When His light shines on those sitting in darkness, it will be like a beacon they can follow to the way of peace.

What a beautiful word picture! Can't you see our Lord shining a lantern into a dark and dreary place, the light of tender mercy and love falling on your loved one?

Pray today that our Lord will shine His light into the darkness of our souls, as well as that of our loved ones, and that we (and they) will rise and following Him in the path of peace.

Now in those days a decree went out from Caesar Augustus, that a census be taken of all the inhabited earth. Joseph also went up from Galilee, from the city of Nazareth, to Judea, to the city of David which is called Bethlehem, because he was of the house and family of David, in order to register along with Mary, who was engaged to him, and was with child. (Luke 2:1, 4, 5 NASB)

God had told Micah that the Messiah would be born in Bethlehem (Micah 5:2) but Mary and Joseph were in Nazareth, 70 or more miles away. Harsh terrain and rough, rock mountains separated the two towns. Without a compelling reason, the couple would never have undertaken such a journey on foot with her delivery imminent.

God, however, had a plan to fulfill, and Caesar was his unwitting assistant. His decree required even Joseph and pregnant Mary to make the trip to Bethlehem. As a result, they walked to Bethlehem and were there in time for Jesus's arrival.

It's amazing when you think about it. Sometimes God uses angels to help the plan unfold, but sometimes He uses pagan emperors. God's ability to work through someone to accomplish His will is not dependent upon their faith status. He can use anything and anyone.

Today, pray that God will speak to our loved ones through every person He puts in their path. Pray, too, that every circumstance of their life will point back to God in such a clear way that they will have no choice but to recognize His hand at work.

And she gave birth to her firstborn son; and she wrapped Him in cloths, and laid Him in a manger, because there was no room for them in the inn. (Luke 2:7 NASB)

The Roman Empire had the most modern of conveniences. There were lavish marble bath houses, aqueducts to provide water, paved roads, and bridges that have lasted for centuries. They did not, however, have telephones, email, or texting. There was no overnight mail delivery. There was also no way for Joseph to make a reservation at a Jerusalem hotel. Instead, the first ones to arrive got the available rooms. By the time Joseph and near-delivery Mary arrived in Jerusalem, all the rooms were taken, so they took whatever shelter they could find.

No room for Jesus. It wasn't that the innkeepers didn't want Joseph and Mary, or that the soon-to-be-born Jesus would be unwelcome. The problem was that all the available space was already filled with other guests.

How very like our hearts, and how easy it is to fill our lives with friends, family, work, even good deeds yet leave no room for Jesus. How crowded is your life? Pray today that we and our loved ones will embrace Christ with first priority and welcome Him into our daily lives.

No room for Jesus?
It's time to make room.

And she gave birth to her firstborn son; and she wrapped Him in cloths, and laid Him in a manger, because there was no room for them in the inn. (Luke 2:7 NASB)

What a lovely picture of our Savior! His young parents had no bed, so they nestled their newborn in the safest place they had available. A manger is a hollowed out stone that is used to hold feed for animals. One miraculous night, a manger also held the Bread of Life that would save the world.

Pray today that our loved ones will hunger for the Bread of Life and will embrace the only One who can satisfy their hunger.

In the same region there were some shepherds, staying out in the fields and keeping watch over their flock by night. (Luke 2:8 NASB)

More than 2000 years later, we still talk about the shepherds. They didn't have a glamorous job, a sophisticated lifestyle, or an enormous bank account. They were not political, athletic, or public service figures. They were none of the things that bring fame today.

They were simply doing the work for which they were responsible, and doing it faithfully even when it was not convenient. They were responsive when God interrupted their work day, and instantly obedient to the divine command. In fact, they obeyed "with haste". No piddling around. No whining. They just obeyed. Perhaps most important, they told everyone they saw about what God had done in their lives. They weren't timid or hesitant about their testimony of faith. They were so certain of their faith that they did not hold back.

That relentless and speedy obedience followed by their fearless testimony, despite Roman soldiers all around, is likely the reason they are included in Scripture today. Simply stated, they did what God said to do.

2000 years from now, will people still talk about your obedient faith walk? Will anyone say, "He/she influenced the world for Christ?" Will you make a lasting difference? Are you growing fruit that lasts?

Pray today that we will have a heart for obedience and actions and words that glorify God. Pray, too, that our loved ones will hear the facts of our encounters with the Lord and recognize truth in the quality of our lives.

In the same region there were some shepherds staying out in the fields and keeping watch over their flock by night. And an angel of the Lord suddenly stood before them, and the glory of the Lord shone around them; and they were terribly frightened. (Luke 2:8, 9 NASB)

The shepherds were not in church, at a Bible study, or in a prayer group. They were not at any of the places where we would expect to receive a message from God. In fact, it seemed that they were perfectly safe from encountering any "religion" at all on that lonely night time hillside. They were simply at work, minding their sheep in the fields. They were probably dirty, stinky, and tired. There doesn't seem to be much to distinguish these shepherds except that they were in the right place at the right time, simply fulfilling their responsibilities.

In the dark of the night, an astounding thing happened. An angel appeared to them and lit up the entire area around them with the glory of God. Needless to say, they were very surprised and terribly frightened.

God doesn't require us to be seeking Him for us to have an encounter with him. We can be minding our own business, like these shepherds, and, when we least expect it, He can rock our world with the light of His glory.

It is called Prevenient Grace - the seeking and saving for which Jesus came. How very like God to start Jesus's earthly mission with an amazing display to the ones who were least likely to be expecting to see His glory.

Today, pray that God will meet with our loved ones right where they are and that they will be both astounded by His glory and changed by His grace.

But the angel said to them, "Do not be afraid... (Luke 2:10a NASB)

Once again, the first words spoken by the angel were "don't be afraid". It is a shocking and unexpectedly glorious sight to see an angel. The angel clearly had arrived from The Boss of the Entire World. The natural response probably should be fear when you come face to face with an emissary from the Creator and Sustainer of the Universe.

The Oxford Dictionary defines fear as "an unpleasant emotion caused by the threat of danger, pain, or harm" and it seems appropriate to be afraid of retribution when sinful man encounters the divine.

There is another kind of fear, however, that is often encouraged in Scripture - the fear of God. The Oxford Dictionary defines it as to "regard (God) with reverence and awe". It also describes this fear as "archaic". Can you believe that? It has gone out of style to respect God and regard Him with awe and reverence!

Perhaps that lack of fear towards God is one of the root causes of rebellion. If not being afraid (fearing danger) is a choice, then being afraid (respect and awe) is too.

Today, take some time to look for evidence of God around you and give him the respect, awe, reverence He deserves. Pray that our loved ones will begin to see God as The Almighty and will fear Him in the archaic way that leaves them trembling in awe.

But the angel said to them, "Do not be afraid; for behold, I bring you good news of great joy which will be for all the people; (Luke 2:10 NASB)

Those poor shepherds were still shaking in their sandals over seeing the angel when they heard even more shocking words. For centuries, God had instructed the Jewish people to keep themselves separate. There were very strict rules about Gentiles in their midst. Adulterers, murders, thieves, sinners of all sorts faced harsh punishment and removal from the community. Theirs was not a completely closed faith, but very restricted.

Suddenly, the angel appeared and began to tell them about good news for ALL the people. It was not just for the Hebrew people, but for Romans, Philistines, Samaritans, Gentiles. The good news was for everyone with no exceptions.

Ponder for a moment about how shocking that must have been. It was not only shocking news, but good news for shepherds who, because of the nature of their work, were often dirty and stinky. They, too, probably found themselves on the outskirts of the religious community.

This news changed everything. Faith in our Lord was for everyone. What amazing joy (in the midst of their surprise) they must have felt!

We still have people groups (both social and ethnic) who are considered "outside" the gospel. The wonderful news is this: ALL means everyone. Christ came for every person on earth, no matter the color of their skin or the degree or type of their sin. There is nothing our loved ones, or their friends, have done that can make them ineligible for God's grace.

Today, thank God that His gospel includes sinners like us. Pray, too, that our loved ones will find such a warm welcome in the body of faith that repentance and restoration are made easier by the grace we extend.

For today in the city of David there has been born for you a Savior, who is Christ the Lord. (Luke 2:11 NASB)

The angels were just full of surprises! Not only was this new baby Messiah born for everyone, He was also specifically born for those shepherds. Their announcement changed faith from a corporate, national experience to an intimate, personal one.

Jesus came for you.

How beautiful those words sound, especially when referring to Jesus. The relationship He came to give us is incredibly personal, astoundingly intimate, and available to everyone, saint and sinner alike.

Christ came for me.

Selah.

(Pause and ponder.)

Pray that our loved ones will encounter people today who have an intimate personal relationship with Christ and that, seeing it, they will want to know Christ in the same way. Pray for willingness to bend the knee before a Holy God come down to earth for them.

For today in the city of David there has been born for you a Savior, who is Christ the Lord. This will be a sign for you: you will find a baby wrapped in cloths and lying in a manger." (Luke 2:11, 12 NASB)

By this time, the shepherds must have been reeling! To give confirmation to the news, the angel gave them a sign. The baby had been born in Bethlehem (just as Micah had prophesied) and could be found wrapped in soft rags in a feed trough. How likely was that?

The shepherds might have hesitated if the baby had been born in the Bethlehem Ritz, but they were totally comfortable with feed troughs. They knew where to find them and wouldn't hesitate to enter there. If God wanted shepherds to be first on the scene to worship the newborn Good Shepherd, (and He did) then He needed to tailor-make His birthplace to ensure the shepherds would be there.

Nothing left to chance. Every detail planned. God perfectly orchestrated events so that those shepherds could meet their Savior on that holy night so long ago. He still arranges meetings with the Almighty with the same precision and care.

Today, pray that God will orchestrate a divine encounter for our loved ones that is so tailor-made for them that there is no way they can miss their Savior.

And suddenly there appeared with the angel a multitude of the heavenly host praising God ... (Luke 2:13 NASB)

Shepherds who watched flocks at night tended to be young unmarried men or older boys. They spent their time with animals in a very harsh terrain and without many of the comforts of city workers, and these young shepherds were not accustomed to glamour or fast living. For a shepherd herding a flock of sheep, slow and careful was the goal, because it was most protective of the sheep. When the sudden occurred, it was usually in the form of danger.

On this holy night, however, the announcing angel appeared suddenly, with astounding news. The dictionary defines suddenly as quickly, unexpectedly. While they were still recovering from this shock, a "multitude of the heavenly host" appeared, also suddenly.

Even though the birth of the Messiah had been foretold by the prophets and the Jewish people longed for Him to come in theory, they had stopped expecting His appearance. They were no longer expecting God to move in a dramatic way, much less for angels to appear.

Perhaps we, and our loved ones, are much the same, going about our business as usual, with no expectations of God's active involvement in our daily life. Today, let's ask for sudden - the unexpected move of God in our lives and the lives of our loved ones. When they least expect an encounter with The Lord, may He speak to their hearts in a way that they can neither ignore nor resist.

This will be a sign for you: you will find a baby wrapped in cloths and lying in a manger."
When the angels had gone away from them into heaven, the shepherds began saying to one another, "Let us go straight to Bethlehem then, and see this thing that has happened which the Lord has made known to us." So they came in a hurry and found their way to Mary and Joseph, and the baby as He lay in the manger. (Luke 2:12, 15, 16 NASB)

The angel told the shepherds of the "sign" for confirmation of his words. The Messiah had been born and they could see Him for themselves as proof. All doubt erased by a babe in a feed trough.

From the very day of His birth, our Lord has provided confirmation for doubters. He is not intimidated or worried by unbelieving, doubting humans but instead provides proof in a gentle, dramatically clear way. It was a way of life for our gentle Savior, this making it easier for us to believe. From shepherds with their flocks to Thomas after resurrection, Jesus offered proof, and still does today.

Pray today that He will reveal Himself to our loved ones with such clarity and confirmation that truth will be unassailable, all their doubts will be wiped away, and they will respond with knees bent in humility and surrender.

"This is what you're to look for: a baby wrapped in a blanket and lying in a manger." As the angel choir withdrew into heaven, the sheepherders talked it over. "Let's get over to Bethlehem as fast as we can and see for ourselves what God has revealed to us." . (Luke 2:12,15 MSG)

Obedience. Sometimes I'm a little slow about it, especially something that disrupts my routine and requires considerable extra effort. The shepherds would have to leave the sheep with minimal security, walk (or run) to Bethlehem, and search through all the caves adjacent to houses for a baby lying in a feed trough. There was no flashing sign. The star had not yet arrived. Their only clue was the feed trough.

These shepherd did not fret, worry, or complain. They didn't try to map out the plan or devise a search strategy. When the angels said go, they went. When they were told to seek the baby, they sought. Not just obedience, but instant obedience.

What wonderful dividends their instant obedience yielded! They were the very first to see the newborn Messiah and his parents. The joy their obedience brought was worth the effort.

What hidden blessings does God have waiting for us to receive when we instantly obey? Oh, what joy could be ours if we, like the shepherds, would move "as fast as we can"!

Today, pray for instant obedience - for ourselves as well as for our loved ones. Pray that we will move in response to the call of God "as fast as we can".

...the sheepherders talked it over. "Let's get over to Bethlehem as fast as we can and see for ourselves what God has revealed to us." They left, running, and found Mary and Joseph, and the baby lying in the manger... (Luke 2:15-16 MSG)

At what point in the shepherds' adventure did belief begin? Where did their faith start? When they saw the angels? During their discussions afterward? When they saw the baby? It wasn't really faith when they just talked a good game. To believe is to accept something as true. Faith means accepting something as true without evidence to prove it. "We should go" does not necessarily mean "I believe what I have just heard is true." Talk became faith when they stood up and started running. That first step toward Bethlehem was a step of pure faith - that the angels they could no longer see were really there, that they had, in fact, heard an angel speak, and that what the angel said was true. They believed as they went.

The easy thing for a child in a faith family is to believe that his parents believe. He sees them live their faith (with all their successes and failures) on a daily basis. It is altogether different to possess faith of your own. The shepherds took hold of their faith as they started running to Bethlehem. They owned it in a way they likely never had before. When our loved ones possess a genuine faith in Christ, it will begin to make a change we can see in their actions, just as our faith has made a change in us. What a beautiful sight it will be to see our loved ones filled with faith and running to Jesus.

Pray today for the mustard seed of faith that will grow our loved ones into faith-runners making their way closer to their Lord.

When they had seen this, they made known the statement which had been told them about this Child. (Luke 2:17 NASB)

They saw the messenger angel, heard the angelic choir, ran to Jesus, and were so astounded by it all that they could not keep quiet. They told everyone they encountered along the way. The shepherds were sharing the Good News, and that should be our response to an encounter with Christ as well.

Pray today that the believers our loved ones encounter today will be so astounded by Jesus and what He has done for them that they will not fail to share their Good News with them.

And all who heard it wondered at the things which were told them by the shepherds. But Mary treasured all these things, pondering them in her heart. (Luke 2:18, 19 NASB)

The shepherds told everyone what they had seen and heard, and Scripture describes two reactions to their news. Almost everyone was amazed (deeply impressed) by the story of their experience. Mary, however, treasured every word of their testimony. We often forget in the midst of the Christmas story, but Mary had paid a terrible price for her obedience. For an engaged girl to become pregnant meant she had been immoral and was impure, and there were severe social consequences for such behavior. In Mary's situation, pregnant as a virgin by the Sprit of God, she was judged as impure despite the truth, and the change in public opinion toward her must have been painful. The miraculous events described by the shepherds gave confirmation to the truth of her virgin pregnancy, and must have felt a little like vindication straight from God. Her response was to treasure and to ponder.

Christmas decorations are up, and the Holy Day is drawing near. As we approach Christmas, let's pray that every mention of the Christmas story will not only be a source of amazement for our loved ones but will stir them to ponder what the birth of the Christ child means for their lives as well.

The sheepherders returned and let loose, glorifying and praising God for everything they had heard and seen. It turned out exactly the way they'd been told! (Luke 2:20 MSG)

The shepherds' run to Bethlehem was one of pure faith that what they had heard on the Judean hillside was true. Their walk back was pure joy because what they had heard WAS true, and had been confirmed by what they saw. There was, indeed, a Baby in a feed trough and He was the Holy One promised by the Prophets, come to save them.

Imagine their overwhelming excitement as they talked together and shared the news with everyone they saw. There was no way they could keep it to themselves! Perhaps you, too, once felt that great joy over finding your Savior. Are you still bubbling over with the joy of meeting your Savior? If not, ask God to restore the joy of your salvation so that you can share with the enthusiasm of the shepherds.

Today we are praying that our loved ones will come face to face with the Babe of Bethlehem and their seeking will find an end in Him. Pray too that the joy of their salvation will be uncontainable.

And when eight days had passed, before His circumcision, His name was then called Jesus, the name given by the angel before He was conceived in the womb. (Luke 2:21 NASB)

Mary and Joseph did exactly what the law required. After eight days, they took the baby for circumcision. Scripture says His name was then called Jesus. In my usual wondering way, I saw this and thought, "what did they call Him before circumcision? Baby? Sweetie Pie?" Maybe the wording actually means that by then they were calling Him Jesus. Regardless, I was on a rabbit trail of wondering about what we call Jesus. According to Cruden's Concordance, 198 different names and titles for Jesus are used in Scripture, raging from Advocate, Redeemer, and Savior to Holy One and Word of Life. There is a song I learned as a child that says "my best friend is Jesus". That's the name I like best. Jesus. Best friend. Closest companion. Lover of my soul.

Jesus once asked Peter, "Whom do you say that I am?" It's a question we all must answer. Of the many names Jesus has been called, whom do you say He is? Today, spend some time thinking about who Jesus is to you, and pray that our loved ones will encounter Him in a fresh way as Savior, Redeemer, Cleanser of souls, Friend.

And when eight days had passed, before His circumcision, His name was then called Jesus, the name given by the angel before He was conceived in the womb. (Luke 2:21 NASB)
For You formed my inward parts; You wove me in my mother's womb. (Psalms 139:13 NASB)

Jesus (being both God and man) was known by name before He was conceived. The amazing thing is that we are also known. The psalmist said that God Himself formed us in our mother's womb. We and our loved ones are the very handiwork of God and known by Him.

There is something so comforting about being known, isn't there? It reminds us that we are not alone. We are not without help in time of trouble. Even more comforting to me is that the One who knit our loved ones together, cell by cell, before they were even born, has a personal investment in their lives.

He knows them.

God knows your loved one and He loves them too. He sees them. They are not forgotten. They are not forsaken.

Praying today that our Lord will continue His work of formation and transformation to draw our loved ones (and us) closer to Him and make us more like Jesus.

and to offer a sacrifice according to what was said in the Law of the Lord, "A pair of turtledoves or two young pigeons." (Luke 2:24 NASB)

But store up for yourselves treasures in heaven, where neither moth nor rust destroys, and where thieves do not break in or steal; (Matthew 6:20 NASB)

God's sense of economy is an interesting thing. Mary and Joseph were carrying Jesus to the temple to present him to The Lord (Numbers 3:13 - Every firstborn son is holy to The Lord) and to present the sacrifice for post-partum cleansing. Their offering was the one given by the poorest people. They were sacrificing birds because they couldn't afford both a bird and a spotless lamb.

What's ironic (and amazing) is that, in their arms, they were carrying THE Spotless Lamb of God who would BE the cleansing sacrifice for their (and our) sins. There was no way they could "afford" such a sacrifice, but God, in a display of His extravagant love, had provided. As they offered the birds for cleansing and the Lamb of God for dedication back to Him, they were bringing the poorest offering and the richest. God had provided, and He was making the payment for their sin with His Son. In God's economy, the poorest (Mary and Joseph) were also the richest. It wasn't the number of shekels they carried that made them rich. It was the Christ Child.

That same sense of divine economy is still at work today. It's not the size of our bank account, the amount in our retirement fund, or the number of square feet in our house that makes us rich. In God's eyes, the amount of fruit we bear for Him is what makes us rich. It's all about relationship. Do we put our trust in things or in Christ?

Pray today for a godly sense of economy and priority. Pray too that our loved ones will turn to Jesus for cleansing and purpose in their lives rather than wealth and the accumulation of things.

And there was a man in Jerusalem whose name was Simeon; and this man was righteous and devout, looking for the consolation of Israel; and the Holy Spirit was upon him. (Luke 2:25 NASB)

Simeon was a wonderful man and we would do well to look at him once more. He was righteous, which means (according to Merriam Webster Dictionary) that he consistently acted in accord with the law. He did what the law required. Righteous implies free from guilt or sin.

Devout, however, tells us that Simeon was committed to his faith both publicly and privately. His faith was real and not just for show. His religion wasn't about the size or number of his sacrifices, it was about his relationship with the Almighty.

In "looking for the consolation of Israel", we see that Simeon was a man of hope and faith. He knew the word of God and believed every bit of it. He wasn't worried that hundreds of years had passed and still no Messiah. Simeon knew what God had promised was exactly what God would do. His feet were in the present but he had his eye on the future. He was expectant, which is the reason he was at the temple at just the right time to see God do exactly what He had said He would.

Even more important, the Holy Spirit rested on Simeon. We might called him "Spirit-filled". He had a personal, ongoing relationship with the Spirit of God and it, more than anything else, directed and defined his life. When the Spirit directed him to the temple, he went. There is no evidence of a struggle about work, family, or civic responsibilities. The Spirit said go, and Simeon went.

Oh how different our lives would be if we had the heart of Simeon! The good news is that we can have the same kind of faith-life Simeon had. By spending time in Bible study, we too can know the promises of God so that we can anxiously await His move. Through prayer and quiet time with our Lord, we can move past just obeying a set of rules to relationship with the Holy One. By submitting to His will, and simply inviting the Spirit into our lives, we too can be filled and directed, empowered and equipped by the Spirit of God.

Now just for a moment, think about the promises you DO know in Scripture, especially the ones like "train up a child..." and "not willing for any to perish"... Make those promises your own, just as Simeon did, and purpose in your heart to hold firm in faith until you see the fulfillment of them from God. You can count on God to do what He has said He would do. The question for today is can God count on you?

Praying today for the heart and faithfulness of Simeon for ourselves and our loved ones

And it had been revealed to him by the Holy Spirit that he would not see death before he had seen the Lord's Christ... Then he took Him into his arms, and blessed God... (Luke 2:26, 28 NASB)

Now to Him who is able to do far more abundantly beyond all that we ask or think, according to the power that works within us, (Ephesians 3:20 NASB)

Maybe it went something like this... Simeon was studying about the Messiah, mostly likely the book of Daniel from which the arrival of the Messiah could be calculated, and he prayed, "Lord, it could be in my lifetime. Would you let me live to see this One you are sending?" At that moment, the Still Small Voice responded. "Yes, Simeon. You will see it." Simeon had counted on that promise ever since. One day, that same Voice whispered, "Go to the temple right now." Simeon knew that voice and he didn't waste a minute. He went.

He saw the Messiah, just as he had asked. Simeon was probably absolutely astounded at seeing the Christ, and he reached out his arms toward Him. Here's where the greatness of our God comes into Simeon's life. Our precious Lord goes one step better. One of the parents quietly handed the Babe to him!! God allowed Simeon to hold the Consolation of Israel in his outstretched arms. He didn't just see. Simeon held Him close to his heart. God gave Simeon more than he had asked, and probably more than he dreamed, when He allowed him to hold the baby Jesus.

He still exceeds. No matter what you have been praying for your loved ones, God can go beyond it. Pray today that our loved ones will go to see and find themselves reaching out for the Christ and drawing Him close to their hearts. Pray too that God will answer our prayers in that wonderful "exceeding abundantly above" way of His... More than we can ask or think.

His father and mother were amazed at the things which were being said about Him. (Luke 2:33 NASB)

Simeon was a devout man who longed to see the Messiah. The Holy Spirit had revealed to him that he would not die before he had seen the Christ. He was constantly on the lookout. One day, the Spirit led him to the temple. What joy and excitement he must have felt! I can just imagine that his heart was pounding and he was wondering, "Can it really be that I will see the Christ today?" Scared and excited, he went as directed and was waiting when young Mary and Joseph arrived at the temple in Jerusalem.

For a young, poor couple from the little village of Nazareth, it must have been overwhelming to walk the packed streets of Jerusalem with an infant. The temple was an incredible building and unbelievably busy. There were crowds of people as well as hordes of animals being brought for sacrifice. Can't you just hear the noise and see the bustle? Mooing, bleating, chirping!

The least expensive animals for the postpartum cleansing sacrifice were the birds (turtledoves or pigeons) and it was all Mary and Joseph could afford. How intimidated they must have been that day as they made their way through the crowds to offer their sacrifice.

Simeon was watching eagerly and, when he spotted them, the Spirit confirmed his deepest desire! This poor couple with the baby did not look like they were carrying "the consolation of Israel", but Simeon did not hesitate. He went straight to them, greeted them, and reached out to hold the baby.

As he held the Babe, he began to prophesy over little Jesus, saying, "I have seen Your salvation, Lord..."

The prophesy continued and Mary and Joseph were amazed at all he said. Mary had seen the messenger angel, heard Elizabeth's prophetic greeting, carried the child, heard the shepherds. The sacrifice they carried was for her. Joseph, on the other hand, had married Mary, despite her pregnancy, in response to a dream, knowing he was not the physical father of her child. Mary was certain of God's hand in their situation, but Joseph had not had as much confirmation. Perhaps he, as most men would, was still harboring uncertainty.

Simeon's words must have been the comfort and confirmation Joseph needed. The shepherds in the night were one thing, but this man was a sophisticated city-dweller who said he had been waiting for Jesus for years.

Amazed.

Utterly, totally amazed.

That's how Joseph felt. All Mary had told him was true. All he had trusted and staked his future on was real. God truly was at work in their situation. Marrying Mary WAS right. In the midst of the emotions he felt, relief must have been paramount!

God knew the hard times Joseph had faced and would face in the future. He knew his fears and his doubts. On that day in Jerusalem, divine orchestration brought the right man with just the right words to just the right spot and God fulfilled the deepest needs of two very different men.

Praying today that our Lord will continue to orchestrate the events of our lives and those of our loved ones so that doubts are washed away, hope is renewed, faith is strengthened, and the Hand of God is confirmed

And Simeon blessed them and said to Mary His mother, "Behold, this Child is appointed for the fall and rise of many in Israel, and for a sign to be opposed- (Luke 2:34 NASB)

"The fall and rise of many". Simeon's wording is odd because the usual way of speaking is "rise and fall". His prophetic wording was exactly right on many levels, however. Jesus Himself demonstrated this when he died on the cross, was buried and resurrected. He fell and rose.

This principle of falling and rising is a hard one for us. We want to rise without falling at all, don't we? Instead, the way of the cross is to die to self, letting go of our sin and willfulness, and rise to new life in Christ, living the way He did - filled with grace and mercy.

If we understood what the falling would do for us, it might not be so hard to willingly relinquish control of our lives to the One who created us and knit us together in the first place. He offers us abundant life and instant contact with the Creator and Sustainer of the Universe, the Lover of our Souls. He offers forgiveness, cleansing, peace, joy, love. He offers a plan for our lives that is good and designed with our best interest in mind. What a wonderful thing to fall and rise!

It is the falling before an Unseen God that is frightening and keeps us from God's best for us. In His plan, however, there is no rising without first falling before Him in humility and repentance.

Perhaps we have areas of our lives in which some falling is needed in order to allow God greater control. Pray today that we will willing humble ourselves before The Worthy One and relinquish those areas to which we are foolishly clinging. Pray, too, that our loved ones will come to the point of surrender, falling before our Lord so that they can be raised to the new life only Christ can give.

there was a prophetess, Anna the daughter of Phanuel, of the tribe of Asher. She was advanced in years and had lived with her husband seven years after her marriage, and then as a widow to the age of eighty-four. She never left the temple, serving night and day with fastings and prayers. (Luke 2:36, 37 NASB)

This is an amazing story in two short verses. Anna married as a young woman. Seven years later, her husband died. Somewhere along the way, she began to live the truth of Isaiah 54:4-5 (your husband is your Maker) and lived as the bride of The Lord. Matthew Henry suggests that she had a small apartment at the temple where she lived, for she "never left the temple" and she served night and day.

She didn't serve by cooking and cleaning for the priests (both good and necessary services) but by prayer and fasting. She understood the importance and the effectiveness of prayer. It was no accident that the arrival of our Savior coincided with the continual prayers of one elderly woman. I suspect those decades of unrelenting prayers were a significant part of ushering in hearts prepared to receive the Christ.

There was a wonderful benefit to her service. As a result of her faithful service (praying night and day in the temple), she was there the day the baby Jesus arrived with His parents. Seeing Him, she began to give thanks to God and didn't stop. She told everyone who was waiting for the Messiah. He has come!

Hearts committed to intercession provide a vital service to The Lord and His church. Our prayers are critical in the kingdom. Do not think that even one of our prayers has gone unheard, nor unanswered. Do not give up hope. Anna had spent years in near continual intercession. There were surely some who disparaged her, but not God. He rewarded her by bringing Jesus straight to her!

We have not yet seen all God will do in our loved ones, but persevere in intercession, dear Ones. Do not fail to offer this lovely service to our Lord. Our prayers are a sweet smelling aroma to Him and He will reward in due time.

Continue to pray today for surrender and transformation for our loved ones.

When they had performed everything according to the Law of the Lord, they returned to Galilee, to their own city of Nazareth. (Luke 2:39 NASB)

It is about 70 miles from Jerusalem to Nazareth, and at least a three day walk (maybe longer carrying an infant). Despite the distance, when they completed what God required of them in Jerusalem, Mary and Joseph headed home to Nazareth. There is no evidence that they considered relocating to Jerusalem. Nazareth was home, so that's where they were going. Joseph's business and their family and friends were there.

The scandal and rumors of an unwed but pregnant teenager were also there. I would have wanted to avoid a lifetime of whispers about me and my son by moving (well, running away), but Mary and Joseph went home to face whatever God allowed. They knew the truth and lived accordingly, no matter what anyone else thought. How freeing it must have been to reject shame and just obey by living the life God had chosen for them! Their greatest desire was pleasing God, not pleasing man, so that's how they lived.

What would our lives be like if our greatest desire was pleasing God no matter the cost? Where would we be located? What kind of work would we do? What choices would we make? What would people say about us? The example of Mary and Joseph teaches us that obedience is what matters, not the consequences that obedience brings. Count the cost, but obey anyway.

Pray today that obedience to the commands of Christ will be our greatest desire, as well as that of our loved ones and that we (and they) will faithfully, unflinchingly walk the path God has for us.

Acknowledgments

Many people helped with this project before I realized there was a project with which to help. My sister, Merry Pennell (aka Cookie), and Missy Lunceford were the first two who joined me in the prayer journey that birthed this book. Lewayne and Susan Lambert were the first to realize I was doing more than daily devotionals, and the first to recognize there was an advent book hidden in those messages. Gene Merkl has been an unbelievable encourager, always having the right word at just the right time. Shelia Matthews has prayed me through everything for years, and has been my intercessor and friend throughout this project, as well. Fred Page has had infinite patience with me as I struggled to balance all the jobs I do and has kept the financials straight, which is a miracle in itself. The daily prayer group, who suffered through texts that were ridiculously long and at insanely early hours, included Jani Bland, Dr. David Eldridge, Jenny Freeman, Marshall Hollis, Wendy Howell, Lisa Kwasinski, Dr. Lewayne and Susan Lambert, Dr. Rocky Livoni, Missy Lunceford, Shelia Matthews, Gene Merkl, Wanda Mitchell, Jan Musgrove, Merry Pennell, Mary Reese, Lori Smith, and Alison Tomes.

My dear son Ryan has helped me with the hyperlinks and marketing, and there is no telling what else he will have done by the time this gets to market! He is ever ready to help and unbelievably patient, and I am extremely grateful for him and to him.

Of course, Jesus is the One who wrote it all. His still small voice whispered these words into my heart in the pre-dawn hours exactly as you see them. All I did was transcribe it.

Thanks to you, dear readers, who trusted the possibility enough to purchase and read this book. May

God exceed your wildest dreams as you allow Him to work in you and through you.

Hearts are breaking throughout the body of Christ as believing parents ask themselves, "What did I do wrong?" I have asked myself that very question at least a thousand times. I don't have all the answers. I wish I did. The good news is that I know Who DOES have all the answers. Scripture is filled with promises for those who love Him, and some of them deal with our children and the choices they make.

The battle for the heart is, at its most basic, a spiritual battle. Ephesians 6:10-18 explains exactly what we are to do, and how we do it. Our only offensive weapon is the word of God, and we are clearly instructed to pray without ceasing. Praying the Word of God in concert with other believers does more than just encourage those who pray. Our Lord promises that, when two or three gather together, He will be with us. It also tells us that, when two or more agree in prayer, our Father will do it. (Matthew 18-19-20)

If you have a prodigal in your life, it can be the most difficult situation imaginable. The redemption of that prodigal becomes the one overriding priority of your life. Take heart! God views it as a priority as well. He is not just ignoring your prayers. He is infinitely patient because He does not want ANY to perish. He does not want YOUR PRODIGAL to perish. 2 Peter 3:9

Parents of Prodigals is a loosely organized group of parents who are deeply committed to praying for their children. Not all of them have children that would be considered prodigals. Some parents are praying for direction and the will of God. Regardless of your prayer need or the faith condition of your child, we invite you to join with us in prayer.

We have found that a group of twelve is ideal. You might find one or two (or twelve) parents to join with you in praying for your children. Prayer guides are posted every morning at www.leannahollis.blogspot.com. You can sign up to receive the devotional/prayer guides by email if you'd like. Plans are underway for additional resources, and a Praying for Prodigals website should be live by December 1, 2013.

Dear ones, it is my prayer for each of you that you will find God active in your life, that you will see His redemption, and that those you love will become the Godliest people you know.

www.ingramcontent.com/pod-product-compliance
Lightning Source LLC
Chambersburg PA
CBHW020519030426
42337CB00011B/472